Children in our World

GLOBAL CONFLICT

Louise Spilsbury

Hanane Kai

BARRON'S

First edition for the United States and Canada published in 2018
by Barron's Educational Series, Inc.

First published in Great Britain in 2016 by Wayland

Wayland is an imprint of Hachette Children's Books, part of Hodder & Stoughton.
A Hachette U.K. company.
www.hachette.co.uk
www.hachettechildrens.co.uk

Text © Hodder & Stoughton, 2016
Written by Louise Spilsbury
Illustrations © Hanane Kai, 2016

Texturing of illustrations by Sarah Habli
Edited by Corinne Lucas
Designed by Sophie Wilkins

All inquiries should be addressed to:
Barron's Educational Series, Inc.
250 Wireless Boulevard
Hauppauge, NY 11788
www.barronseduc.com

ISBN: 978-1-4380-5021-8

Library of Congress Control No.: 2017944956

Date of Manufacture: November 2017
Manufactured by: WKT Co., Ltd., Shenzhen, China

Printed in China
9 8 7 6 5 4 3 2 1

The website addresses (URLs) included in this book were valid at the time of going to press.
However, it is possible that contents or addresses may have changed since the publication of this
book. No responsibility for any such changes can be accepted by either the author or the Publisher.

Contents

People in conflict

People around the world belong to different groups. They can be part of a family, a school, and maybe a club or team, too. People also come from different countries and religions. Most of the time different groups live side by side and in peace.

4

People don't always get along, though. When they don't, they come into conflict. They may fight or try to hurt each other. When we see news about conflicts around the world it can make us feel sad, angry, and scared. This book will help you make sense of what's happening.

Why do conflicts happen?

When people argue, they can usually solve their problems fairly quickly by talking and coming up with a solution. Conflicts happen when groups of people or countries cannot solve their problems by talking, and they start fighting instead. Conflicts may also happen when one group or country tries to take land from another, or when people fight to stop others from being hurt or from being treated badly.

Some people think that everyone should live the same way that they do. They may try to get other people to share their beliefs and customs. If they try to force other people to follow their rules, this can also cause conflict and violence.

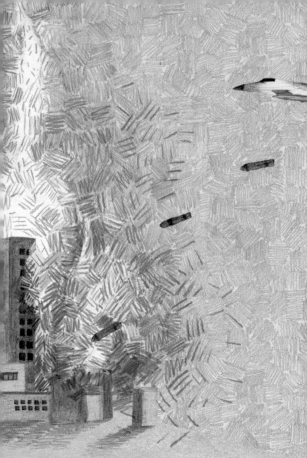

What is war?

During a war, different groups battle with each other until one side gives up or loses. Sometimes the war stops because they've been able to talk through their problems. Leaders decide how, where, and when to fight their enemy. Soldiers attack each other using weapons and bombs. People from both sides who do not fight in the war are called civilians.

Most people believe that war is bad, and that it is better to solve problems by talking. But sometimes people go to war because they think it is the only way to stop bad things from happening. Soldiers who fight in wars do so to protect the things and people they care about.

What is terrorism?

Terrorism is when people carry out acts of violence to get attention for their ideas and aims. Terrorists are people who feel badly treated or disagree with other people's beliefs. Sometimes terrorists act alone, and other times they are part of a bigger group. Terrorists hide and use bombs and other weapons to hurt people in public places, such as airports and train stations.

Terrorists want to scare people to get world leaders to do what they want. But, it's important to remember that the chances a terrorist will hurt you or the people you love are very, very small.

What happens in conflicts?
People on both sides of a conflict can be injured or killed during war and terrorist attacks. Homes and belongings may be ruined during fighting. The places where people work, worship, or study may be burned down or destroyed.

Sometimes people leave their homes to escape terrible fighting or
violence. They go to find a safer place to live and to have a better life.
People who leave their home country because their lives are in danger
are called refugees.

Changing lives

Conflicts can change people's lives forever. People have to find new homes, and roads, bridges, and buildings need to be repaired. Refugees have to find somewhere new to live and work. They also have to make new friends and often learn new languages. After a conflict, people may feel scared and sad for a long time.

Imagine not being able to go to school. When schools are destroyed, children lose the chance to learn and play together. So, teachers may give classes in unusual places until a new school is built.

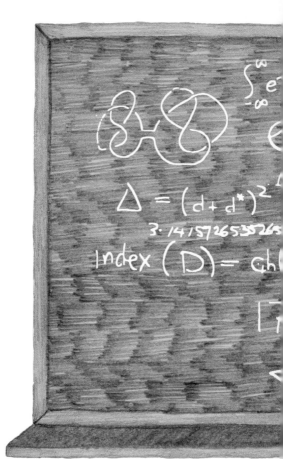

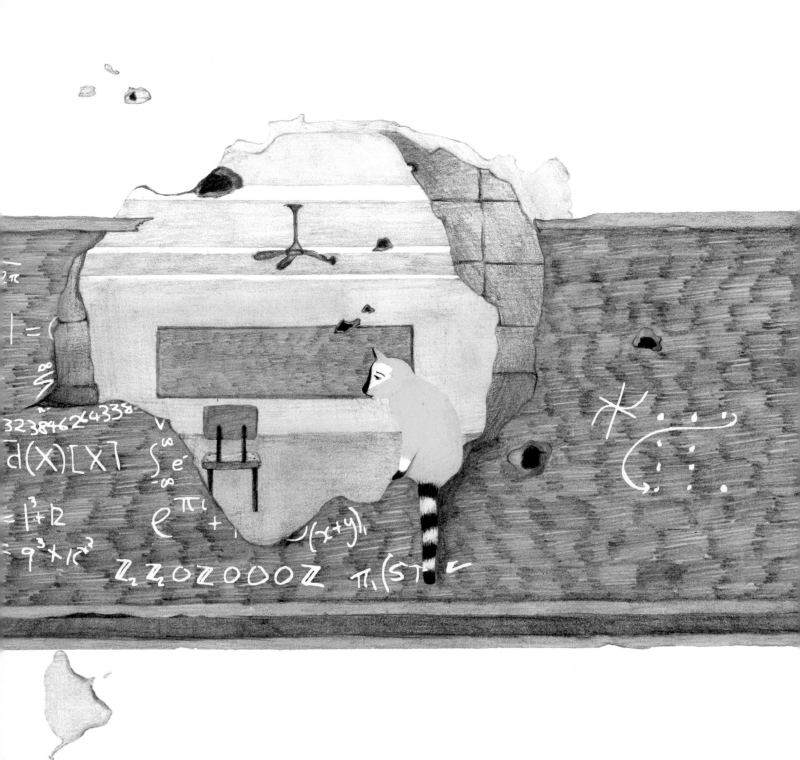

People who help

A charity is a group that helps people in need. Charity workers bring clean water, food, blankets, and tents to people who have lost their homes. They comfort people who are upset. They bring doctors, nurses, and medicine to help people who are hurt.

Governments and charity workers also help people get their lives back to normal. They find homes for refugees and pay for the materials needed to make new buildings and repair power lines. They also bring tools and machines so people can work again.

Keeping people safe

Rules keep us safe. At school there are rules to stop you from hitting or bullying others. The world also has a set of rules, or laws, about what happens in war. These laws protect children, civilians, injured soldiers, hospitals, and places of worship.

Most people obey these laws during war. If they do not,
they can be punished. They may be put in prison for
their crimes. Some countries may stop buying
from and selling to a country that breaks
war laws. This can make a country obey
the laws again.

Ending conflicts

It's good if you can solve arguments on your own, but sometimes you may need an adult's help. There are people who help solve world conflicts, too. The United Nations is a group of countries that work together to end wars and protect civilians.

The United Nations and world leaders try to get the two sides in a war to talk. They help different groups find a fair way to resolve their problems without hurting each other or other people. They try to solve problems with words, not weapons.

Avoiding conflicts

It is normal for people to disagree sometimes. The important thing is not to let an argument turn into a fight. It helps if people can stay calm and say what they think in a polite, friendly way. If people shout and say mean things, both sides can lose their temper.

If everyone listens carefully to each other, it helps them understand how they each feel. Then, they can come to a compromise. That's when each group gives up something to come to an agreement—like when sports teams agree to share a field rather than fight over it.

Understanding others

One way to avoid conflicts is to better understand each other. We are all the same in a lot of ways. We all need a home, food, water, family, and friends. We all deserve to be safe and to choose our own beliefs. Understanding others helps us to be respectful to each other and live together in peace.

It is natural to feel angry when we see people being treated poorly. But, we shouldn't blame a whole group of people when a few people do something wrong. If one student stole a computer from your school, it would be wrong to say that all of the children in your school were thieves, wouldn't it?

Talk about it

It's good to learn and care about world conflicts, but it's bad to worry about them too much. If you are upset, talk to an adult you trust about how you feel. He or she can help you. It also helps to think about what's good in the world and to do things that you enjoy, like playing with friends.

Most people are caring and kind. The main reason we see conflicts in the news is that they don't happen very often. You and your family are not at a great risk of danger. Remember: There are a lot of clever people working to stop wars and terrorism to make the world a safer place for us all.

How can you help?

It feels good to help people. There are lots of things you could do. You could collect food or clothes to give to refugees. You could have a bake sale or put on a show to raise money for charities that help people in conflicts. Or, you could write a letter to the government asking them to help. What ideas do you have?

Find out more

Books

The Forgiveness Garden
Lauren Thompson, Feiwel & Friends, 2012

Four Feet, Two Sandals
Karen Lynn Williams, Eerdmans, 2016

The Journey
Francesca Scanna, Flying Eye Books, 2016

Websites

The Red Cross is a charity that helps victims of war and disaster.
www.redcross.org

The UN Refugee Agency (UNHCR) works to protect
and assist refugees worldwide.
www.unhcr.org

War Child Canada helps children in war-affected
communities by providing education, opportunity,
and justice.
www.warchild.ca

Glossary

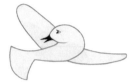

charity a group that helps people in need

civilian a person who is not in the army

compromise when two sides both give up something to come to an agreement

conflict a very angry disagreement, fight, battle, or war

custom something that a group of people regularly does together

government a group of people who control and make decisions for a country

refugee a person who leaves his or her home country to find a safer place to live

religion a belief in a god or gods, for example, Islam and Christianity

respect to care about other people's feelings and opinions

terrorist a person who uses weapons and other violent acts to scare people

United Nations a group of countries that work together to prevent and end wars

worship to show respect for a god, for example, to pray

Index